The Dig!

---

101 Questions in
Consciousness

Rowena E. Silvera

ISBN: 1466453656
ISBN-13: 978-1466453654

DEDICATION

To (*in order of appearance*):

Spirit for a wonderful opportunity to explore and create.

My parents for life, love and lineage — my mother would tell me: "It doesn't belong to anyone, more than it belongs to you!" I have learned how to live into that gift of consciousness.

My sisters for love, protection, support and blasts of color! You were my first idols...

My family: Nephews, Nieces, Step-children and all — thanks for "getting" me.

My sister-friends (old & new) for the laughs, the meals, the late nights, listening to yet "Just one more idea/invention," the love and for "walking" with me from Harlem to the Village and working it all out... "Nobody else got it, but I knew you would..."

My husband, oh where do I begin? Thank you for real love... 4, Boulevard Raspail?

ADT & Kairos Family: You both really did "have me at hello."

The Five Darlings: Rain, music, art literature and questions

And finally,

To all the other players: Joys, Challenges, Breakdowns and Breakthroughs – it's all good 'cause it's all God!

Rowena E. Silvera.

Your visions will become clear
only when you can look into your own heart.
Who looks outside, dreams;
who looks inside, awakes.

— C.G. Jung

CONTENTS

INTRODUCTION

After a tumultuous period almost 30 years ago, I experienced an emotional impasse and was desperate for healing. I continually asked myself, "Why do I feel this way?" but no answer came. I persisted with the question for almost a year: "Why do I feel this way?" Eventually I received an answer, "Your thinking is *ALL* wrong!"

"Great!" I thought, "What does that mean?" "What am I supposed to do about the way I think?" I can't help what goes on in my mind—it's just the way I think...

Time passed and nothing changed. I kept thinking about the words: "Your thinking is *ALL* wrong!" What did that mean?

Some months later, as I was walking in nine inches of Brooklyn snow one bright winter morning I could feel an answer emerging: *"You are trying to perform from an old script, but you don't believe your lines. Find your own truth and you will find a life that you can believe in,* but *you are going to have to **dig**..."*

INTRODUCTION

Finding my own truth seemed like sound advice. Almost everyone around me was on track and they were doing extremely well. Despite my best effort, I could not keep up. The truth is, I was not interested in the "track," but I could see no alternative and I craved normalcy. I just wanted to "fit in" and I was not "fitting in" at all. I was *sticking out*—and not in a good way. At that time I would have gladly taken off and studied in a monastery far, far away, but my escapist fantasies were not to be. My life was not set up that way and I was too scared to go off the grid.

With no idea of how to unravel the ball of yarn that had become my very complicated life, I began to implode—becoming depressed, sluggish and despondent. The call to change my thoughts was an opening, and the day in the snow made me realize that I was going to have to stay right there in Brooklyn and begin to *dig* myself out of the mess I was making.

The snow represented my life, expansive and bland, but holding a promise of spring underneath. The questions became my shovel, a shovel that I would carry with me for the rest of my life. Anytime I have a personal challenge I "*dig*" it out with a question or two or six…

INTRODUCTION

Even though at that time the thought of questioning myself felt crazy, I knew that if I wanted to heal I would have to *dig* and questions were the only shovels that I owned.

I began with basics. I needed to question how well I knew myself. Why did I respond to life in the way that I did? Was I acting deliberately or unconsciously? How well did I really know myself?

My political party is the same party of my family and most of my friends. Why? If I were born into another family and had different friends would I be just as comfortable with another ideology? My religion, my taste in food, literature, music are all influenced by my surroundings, certainly enhanced by life experiences, but my core belief system was handed to me.

How would my life change if I really knew myself, if I didn't assume that I knew myself? If the things I took as my beliefs were held under the light of my own interrogation would they survive? I began to survey my thoughts with questions that ranged from the deeply emotional to the silly. The answers often surprised me.

INTRODUCTION

We arrive at a certain age and feel we know ourselves fairly well. We do not question our thoughts; we just live *out* of them. The material world is a creation of these thoughts. It is an emblem of who we are, yet we are not always satisfied with the substance of our existence.

I believe that the more questions we ask ourselves, the more we challenge ourselves. Consider yourself an explorer searching for answers. This is an opportunity for personal archaeology. What treasures will you find? What dust needs to be blown off? What has broken beyond repair? What needs to be discarded?

Many of the questions contained within this book came from that day in the snow and many more I would ask myself over the next quarter century. Still there are more that I have not included in this volume. These questions can be used for group dialogue or workshops. I hope you will use them to weed your own garden and light a fire for creative thought and personal liberation. Some of the questions require deep thought, some will make you laugh, others will give birth to more questions, and still others will leave the proverbial "pebble in your shoe."

INTRODUCTION

I suggest you acquire a journal for your thoughts and for answering the questions in *The Dig!* You don't have to approach the questions in one sitting or even in order; just find a question that resonates with you and set out upon the path toward clarity: contemplate and write.

You have everything you need for this journey. Your answers are within…

Rowena E. Silvera
Winter 2012

1. YOU

Who are you?

What qualities define you?

What limitations do you possess?

How old are you chronologically?

How old are you in your mind?

Is there a difference between your physical age and your mental age?

What accounts for the differences in the *ages*?

1. YOU

Are you paranoid?

Do you take any responsibility for the negative events that occur in your life, or are you the victim of unfortunate circumstances?

Do you think unfortunate things happen to you more often than to other people? If so, why?

If so, why do you think bad things happen to you?

Can you do anything to change that dynamic between you and life?

Are you actively working to change, or are you content with the way you navigate your relationships?

1. YOU

If you could change the family that you were born into, keeping some of your biological family and mixing and matching the rest, would you?

Whom would you keep?

Whom would you switch out and why?

2. VERSIONS OF YOU

Is this the best version of "you" possible?

If so, how do you know that for sure?

If not, why?

What are you doing to become the best "you" possible?

3. FEAR

What are you most afraid of?

How did you develop this fear?

How often does this fear impact your life and in what ways?

How are you going to eliminate this fear from your life?

4. REGRET

What is your biggest regret?

Did it involve a person, an event, or a piece of advice?

Why is it your biggest regret?

Is there anything that you can or want to do about it?

If so, what?

Are you doing it?

4. REGRET

If you have adult children, what is the one piece of advice you regret not giving them?

5. TRIUMPH

What is your greatest triumph?

Describe the event and the impact it had or has on your life.

6. PERSONAL SHORT-TERM IMPACT

What would have the most positive, immediate impact on your life right now?

How do you know it would have the most impact?

How are you securing this agent of change?

7. PERSONAL LONG-TERM IMPACT

What would have the most long-term and far-reaching impact on your life?

How do you know it would have the most impact?

How are you securing this agent of change?

8. RELATIONSHIP WITH MISTAKES

How do you define a mistake?

What is your relationship with mistakes?

What does a mistake say about you?

Do you get over them quickly, or does the "sting" linger for a long time?

If the "sting" lingers, what can you do free yourself from the pain?

9. REPEATED MISTAKES

What is the number one mistake you have repeated most often over the course of your life?

What drives the repetition of this mistake?

What are the second and third biggest mistakes that you have repeated most often over the course of your life?

What drives the repetition of these mistakes?

What is the single-biggest mistake that you have ever made?

Did it have a negative, lasting impression on your life?

9. REPEATED MISTAKES

If so, were you ever able to "course correct" it?

10. NEGATIVE IMPACT

What person, dead or alive, has had the most negative impact on your life?

Why?

Have you eclipsed the impact he or she has had on you?

If so, how?

If not, why and what do you plan on doing about it?

11. POSITIVE IMPACT

What person, dead or alive, has had the most positive impact on your life?

Have you said thank you?

If he or she is alive and you have not said thank you, what are you waiting for?

12. MONEY

What is your relationship with money?

How did this relationship develop?

Does it need to change?

If so, in what ways does it need to change?

How can you take responsibility for its change?

13. EMBARRASSMENT

How do you define embarrassment?

What creates embarrassment?

Do you embarrass easily? Why?

How long does it take you to get over embarrassment?

Do you think that is a healthy amount of time?

If not, why? What do you plan to do about it?

14. GIFTS

What is your greatest gift?

How are you sure it is your greatest gift?

15. YOUR CALLING

Have you been called to the planet to do something?

If so, what is it?

Are you doing it? If not, why?

16. FLAWS & HABITS

What is your biggest flaw?

Do you have any bad habits?

How have your flaws and bad habits impacted your life?

Have your flaws and bad habits impacted the lives of others?

Are you doing anything to remedy your imperfections?

If not, why?

17. CONTROL

Do you get any joy or spark out of controlling others?

If so, why?

Is your need to control healthy or excessive?

If unhealthy, what are you doing or planning to do about it?

Do you have control in your own life?

Is it excessive or balanced?

If unbalanced, what are you doing to balance it?

18. PLEASING OTHERS

Do you get any joy or sense of self-accomplishment out of pleasing others? If so, why?

Is your need to please healthy or excessive?

Do you see yourself as a victim of other people's needs and desires?

If so, how was this relationship created, and how do you plan to change it?

Do you value the opinion of others more than you value your own opinion?

If so, why?

18. PLEASING OTHERS

What are you doing to add a feeling of importance to your own thoughts and opinions?

19. ABANDONMENT

Do you have a fear of abandonment? If so, why?

Who has abandoned you?

Why do you think he or she abandoned you?

Do you think he or she would agree with your conclusion?

Why or why not?

Have you abandoned anyone? If so, why?

Have you apologized or sought forgiveness? Why or why not?

20. FORGIVENESS

What is your general policy on forgiveness?

How was it formed?

Do you stick with your policy, or does it change depending on the offense?

Do you need to forgive anyone? If so, whom and why?

Are you actively engaging in a forgiveness exercise with him or her?

If not, what are you waiting for?

20. FORGIVENESS

Do you need to be forgiven?

Whom would you like to forgive you and why?

21. THE BEST DECISIONS

What are the three best decisions that you have ever made?

How have they impacted the fabric of your life?

22. THE WORST DECISIONS

What are the three worst decisions that you have
ever made?

How have they impacted the fabric of your life?

23. ADVICE FOR THE FORMER YOU

If you could travel back in time and give yourself three pieces of advice, what would the advice be in order of importance?

At what age would you be when you distilled each piece of advice?

24. ADDICTIONS

Do you have any addictions?

How did you become addicted?

If you are still addicted, why do you remain addicted?

25. FILM

What is your favorite movie?

What about the story, the writing, or the performance captured you?

Do you relate to one of the characters in particular?

If so, whom and why?

26. QUOTES

What are your three favorite quotes?

Why are they meaningful to you?

Do you have a personal motto? If so, what is it?

If someone had to quote you as saying one thing most often, what would that quote or sentiment be?

27. MUSIC

What is your favorite song?

What is it about the lyrics and/or the music that resonates with you?

How does it make you feel when you hear it?

28. FAMILY FAVORITE

Who is your favorite living person (relative)?

What meaning has he or she brought to your life?

29. OTHER FAVORITE

Who is your favorite living person (non-relative)?

Why?

What meaning has he or she brought to your life?

30. FAVORITE PERSON OF CELEBRITY

Who is your favorite celebrity, historical person, politician, etc.?

Why?

What qualities do you see in that person(s) that are admirable?

Does he or she have any evident qualities that you'd like to possess?

31. EARLIEST MEMORIES

What is your earliest memory?

What did it teach you?

Has it had a lasting impact on your life?

If so, why?

32. WORST MEMORY

What is your worst memory? What did it teach you?

Has it had a lasting impact on your life?

If so, why?

33. BEST MEMORY

What is your best memory?

What did it teach you?

Has it had a lasting impact on your life?

If so, why?

How have these memories shaped you?

For better or for worse?

34. A SUPREME BEING

Do you believe in a supreme being? If so, why?

Do you have an opinion on people who do not believe in a supreme being?

If you do not believe in a supreme being, why?

If not, do you have an opinion on people who do believe in a supreme being?

35. AFTERLIFE

Do you believe in an afterlife? If so, why?

What would it look like?

Does everyone get to go?

Do you have an opinion on people who do not believe in an afterlife?

If you do not believe, why?

Do you believe in a hell?

If so, where does it exist?

36. THE MEANING OF LIFE

What is the meaning of life?

If you know, how do you know?

Do you want to take a guess at what the meaning and purpose is?

If you don't know, but you could be given the answer under the condition that you could not tell anyone else, would you want to know?

37. WHY ARE YOU HERE?

Why are you on this planet?

Was your arrival an act of biology, or something more?

Explore thoughts about your incarnation.

38. NOW AND HAPPY

Why are you where you are right at this very moment (the room, the airport, the bus, etc.)?

Are you happy to be there?

Are you generally optimistic? If so, how do you maintain an optimistic outlook?

39. YOU AND THE PLANET

Are you a generally negative or positive force on the planet?

Explain your choice.

40. EMOTIONS

Do you control your emotions well?

Would others agree with your assessment?

If you are not in control of your emotions, how does it affect you and those around you?

How long have you been out of control of your emotions?

Are you working toward actively gaining control?

If so, what are you doing?

If not, why?

41. LISTENING

Are you a good listener?

If so, are you sure?

And how do you know?

If not, why?

Do you get bored, or do you have something more important to say?

Can you listen without interjecting and then respond?

Are you compassionate? If so, how are you sure?

Why is compassion important?

Have you ever lacked compassion?

If so, do you remember why you lacked compassion?

Do you regret it?

42. SOUL MATES

Do you believe in soul mates?

Why or why not?

If so, do you have a soul mate?

Do you think soul mates are always romantically connected?

Can you have more than one soul mate?

43. LOVE AT FIRST SIGHT

Do you believe in love at first sight?

Why or why not?

If so, has it ever happened to you?

Is it possible to love more than one person with the same intensity at the same time?

Is monogamy natural or a construct of society? If so, why?

44. MOTIVATION

What motivates you the most? Why?

Are you generally self-motivated, or do you need a catalyst to get you "going"?

45. OBLIGATION

Aside from family members and your employment, are you obligated to anything or anyone?

Does obligation make you feel worn down or valuable?

46. SIX MINUTES

If you had six minutes to live (but by some greater force you were not in a panic over it) and six people to call, with the ability only to spend one minute with each person, who are the people you would call?

In what order would you call them and why?

If you could commit one crime in that same six minutes, what would you do and why?

47. FRIENDSHIP

Do you have any friendships that you maintain from childhood?

Who are they, and why are they still in your life?

What is the best quality a friend can have?

Are you a good friend?

Are you sure?

If so, what makes you a good friend?

If not, what makes you lacking?

Are you attempting to approach friendship differently? If so, how?

48. CHILDHOOD

Did you have a good childhood?

If so, why do you classify it as good?

If not, how would you classify it?

What could have made it better?

49. CONNECTIONS

Do you regret losing touch with anyone?

Why did you lose touch?

Will you attempt to reconnect with him or her?

If yes, why?

If no, why not?

50. INFLUENCE

Do you influence anyone (aside from your children)?

Whom?

How did you come to hold influence over him or her?

51. YOUR IMPACT

Have you made an impact on anyone in a positive way?

How?

Have you made an impact on anyone in a negative way?

How?

52. YOU & OTHERS

Are you good with watching the words and attitude you use when engaging others?

If so, how do you know that you appear in a kind and appropriate way?

If not, what behavior do you demonstrate with others that needs to be changed?

What are you actively doing to behave differently?

53. SELFISHNESS

Are you selfish?

If so, how has selfishness impacted your life?

Are you doing anything to become less selfish?

If so, what are you doing?

If not, why?

54. GIVING

Are you giving?

Do you give without regret?

Do you give *past* your comfort zone?

If so, what enables you to "stretch"?

If not, do you think you should learn how to exercise the "giving muscle" more?

55. THE GREATEST TEACHER

Who is or was the greatest teacher that ever lived?

What did he or she teach that left the most impact on the world?

56. A VOTE

If the majority of the people you know had to come together and describe you, what would they consider your greatest gifts?

What would they consider your major challenges?

Why?

57. SUICIDE

Do people have the right to take their own lives?

Why or why not?

58. HUMOR

Who is the funniest person you know?

What makes him or her funny?

Do you have a good sense of humor?

If so, what contributes to your sense of humor?

Do other people find you funny?

59. WELFARE

Do you believe in a public welfare system?

Why or why not?

If you do believe in a public welfare system, should there be a cap on benefits?

If so, how many years?

If a person cannot find employment after the expiration of benefits, what should happen to him or her?

If he or she has children, what should happen to the children?

60. YOUR GOVERNMENT

What would you change about the government under which you live?

Why?

61. DEATH PENALTY

Do you believe in the death penalty?

If not, why?

If so, why?

Could you be the executioner if necessary?

62. GLOBAL IMPACT

What has the most impact on the most people at one time?

63. INTELLIGENCE

Are you intelligent?

How do you know for sure?

How does the answer to this question make you feel?

64. EMOTIONAL HEALTH

Do you maintain good emotional health?

If so, what techniques do you employ?

Where did you learn these skills?

If not, what can you do to change the way you care for your emotional self?

Will you make these changes? Why or why not?

65. ANGER

Do you anger easily?

If so, what do you plan to do about it?

66. BULLYING

What is your view on bullying?

Do you think it is more prevalent now, or has it always existed in the same way, but was accepted as a product of growing up?

Do you think child bullies become adult bullies?

Do you think children that are bullied remain victims of aggression?

Can anything be done about bullying?

If so, what?

Were you ever bullied or a bully?

If so, how has it affected your life?

67. MAGIC

If magic were possible, which would be better—
magic or discipline? Why?

68. POWER

If you had the option of having the power to make things happen instantly with a thought, would you want that power?

Why or why not?

If so, what are the top ten things you would manifest?

If you could pick only one other person in the world to have that same power, whom would it be and why?

69. KINDNESS/FAIRNESS & LIES

Is kindness overrated?

What is more important—kindness of fairness?
Why?

When is it good to tell a lie?

Does what you lie about matter, or is lying the same
across the board?

70. INJUSTICE

What drives injustice?

Can anything be done to stem the tide of injustice?

If yes, what can be done?

71. PEACE

Is world peace possible?

Is it desirable?

Are there any negative effects that could be caused by a world at peace?

72. DESPOT REMOVAL

If you could remove only one despot in history and all the harm done under that regime, who would it be?

Why?

73. DISEASE

If you could cure only one disease, what would it be?

Why?

If you got a chance to do it again, what is the second disease that you would cure?

Why?

74. INVENTION

What is the single greatest invention ever?

Why did you make that choice?

What are the second and third greatest inventions ever?

Why did you make that choice?

If you could invent anything that you wanted, what would it be and why?

75. THE GREATEST ELEMENT

Assuming we could breathe without air and survive without water, which of the four elements: air, fire, earth, or water is the greatest?

Why?

76. RACE & RELIGION

If the world consisted of one race and one religion, would bias and prejudice end or lessen?

77. IF MONEY DID NOT MATTER...

If money were no object, what would you do to occupy your time?

If you are currently employed, would you quit your job?

If so, why?

What would you do with your money?

Are you more motivated by money or personal fulfillment?

If you had to have a second job in addition to your current one but could not be paid for doing it, what job would you choose?

Why?

78. LIVING FOREVER

If you, but only you could live forever, would you want to?

If so, why? If not, why?

79. BIRTH & DEATH

If you could pick or know the date of your death, would you want to?

If you could change the date of your birth, would you?

If so, why?

Do you believe you had anything to do with planning your life in a pre-incarnate stage?

If so, why do you think that?

What, if any, evidence do you have?

80. REINCARNATION

Do you believe in reincarnation?

Why or why not?

81. FLYING & SWIMMING

If you could fly or swim underwater without breathing, which would you choose and why?

82. THE NEXT BEST RELIGION IS...

Aside from your own, what is the next-best religion in the world?

Why?

83. THE SMART PILL

If you could ingest a pill that would give you extensive knowledge on one subject, what would that subject be?

What would you use the knowledge to accomplish?

84. A QUESTION OF TIME

Are you tardy or punctual?

If tardy, why?

Do you think your tardiness breeds resentment in other people?

What, if anything, will you do to change that behavior?

85. YOUR FAVORITES

What is your favorite fruit?

What is your favorite color?

What is your favorite day of the week?

86. YOUR BEST YEAR

What was your best year so far?

Why?

87. JOBS

What are the three most important jobs in society?

Why?

88. BODY PARTS

If you could sell a body part for money, would you?

If so, what part?

How much would you sell it for?

Would you repeat the exercise if you wanted more money?

89. PLAYING A GAME

If you had to play a single round of one game every day for the rest of your life, what would it be?

90. TRUST

Are you a trusting person?

Whom do you trust the most and why?

Do you trust him or her with everything (from secrets to money)?

Can you be trusted with everything (from secrets to money)?

If not, why?

91. RELIABILITY

Who is the most solid and reliable person you know?

What makes him or her solid and reliable person?

Are you a solid and reliable person?

If so, why do you describe yourself as such?

If not, why?

92. LONELINESS

Why are some people lonely in a crowd?

Have you ever been lonely in a crowd?

If so, why did the connection with the people around you fail?

Does this happen to you often?

If so, why?

Are you doing anything to feel more integrated in social situations?

93. FREE WILL

Do animals have free will?

If so, how do you know?

Does nature have a free will?

If so, how do you know?

94. ADOPTION

Can a person love an adopted child as much as a birth child?

Explain your thoughts either way.

How did you come to this conclusion?

95. TECHNOLOGY

If we lost cell phone and Internet use for the next one hundred years, would it create chaos or more balance?

96. THE GREATEST SOCIAL ILL

What is the greatest social ill?

How has it impacted society at large?

Is there anything that can be done to correct that ill?

97. TIME TRAVEL

If you could travel in time in either direction but could not return to the present, would you go?

If so, why?

If not, why?

If you could take someone with you, would you?

What gift would you take from the present to another time in history or the future?

98. A PARALLEL UNIVERSE

Does a parallel universe exist?

If so, how does it operate?

Are you the same "you" but slightly different?

How old are you in that realm?

Would you trade this existence for your "other" existence for a few days without knowing how that other "you" lives?

If so, why?

If not, why?

99. THE KNOWN WORLD

If you could live anywhere in the known world for a year, where would you go?

Whom would you take and why?

100. EDUCATION

What is your highest level of education?

Are you educationally satisfied?

If so, has it brought you the success and/or
fulfillment that you expected?

If you could go back as many years as you'd like,
would you have chosen a different course of study?

If you are not educationally satisfied, what stopped
you from obtaining more education?

Is your reasoning truthful and good?

101. LIFE LESSON

What major life lessons have you learned in the past twenty years?

How do you use them in your current existence?

If you had to whisper one sentence to a baby that he or she would carry with him or her for a lifetime, what would you say and why?

CONCLUSION

Congratulations! You have come to the end—or perhaps the beginning. Now, one more question. How do you feel? I know some of you reviewed every question, perhaps others jumped around a bit and still others decided not to be bothered with the journey at all, saving the trek for another day.

If some questions left you feeling *raw*, open or vulnerable, it's okay. Thoughts only have the power that you give them, but perhaps those sensitive places are the areas where you need the most healing. This collection of questions has presented an opportunity for a continued and extended expedition within.

If you came across a question and you felt your body respond with a "don't go there," it may be worth *going there*, but not alone. Sometimes we should not enter scary and dark places without a guide to shine a light or who can help us navigate our way back out of a cave.

When climbers attempt mountains like K2 or Everest they employ the assistance of sherpas who know the region, the mountains, and the resources necessary to have a successful climb. Our lives can sometimes feel like we are attempting an emotional Everest, so I encourage you to find a "sherpa" of your own. See qualified support in the form of a life coach, a therapist, or a spiritual guide.

We can always control our thoughts by questioning them. Once a spiritual teacher told me, "you don't have to believe everything you think." I learned to speak back to my thoughts, especially when the messages flashing are not life giving, peaceful or empowering. You don't have to fear your thoughts, but you have to manage them. Questions help you to do that. If your thoughts are good and positive they thrive and expand with questions. If they are limiting and harmful, they wither under examination. Speak to your thoughts, for they are speaking to you. Be firm and clear:

"I see you and I hear you, but I will not give you my energy or attention."

"I am not engaging you unless you have uplifting and wise information to provide."

Or simply:

"No, I'm not letting you in…"

Questions! offer an opportunity for forgiveness. At times we need to release others and often we need to release ourselves. You may also realize that you are bound by your past and that every day provides a chance to "get it right." Do not use you answers to further imprison yourself, use them as a door to freedom, to love more deeply, to create beauty with abandon and live out of your very best self.

Your answers may change from year to year, maybe even from reading to reading, as they should. Yet the willingness to *dig* deep, be honest, and face your own truths will make your journey all the more interesting.

I hope you will send me a note about your Dig! I look forward to hearing from you.

thedigbooks@hotmail.com

Add the word "Brooklyn" in the subject line and I will know it is from you!

—Rowena

ABOUT THE AUTHOR

Rowena E. Silvera is a former columnist and contributing editor for a national magazine. She currently serves as the spiritual director of *A Different Thought: A Community Church for Conscious Living* and as administrative director for *The Kairos Institute* based in the metropolitan Atlanta area.

NOTES ON MY DIG!

Question #: _____

NOTES ON MY DIG!

Question #: _____

NOTES ON MY DIG!

Question #: _____

NOTES ON MY DIG!

Question #: _____

NOTES ON MY DIG!

Question #: _____

NOTES ON MY DIG!

Question #: _____

NOTES ON MY DIG!

Question #: _____

NOTES ON MY DIG!

Question #: _____

NOTES ON MY DIG!

Question #: _____

NOTES ON MY DIG!

Question #: _____

NOTES ON MY DIG!

Question #: _____

NOTES ON MY DIG!

Question #: _____

NOTES ON MY DIG!

Question #: _____

NOTES ON MY DIG!

Question #: _____

NOTES ON MY DIG!

Question #: _____

NOTES ON MY DIG!

Question #: _____

NOTES ON MY DIG!

Question #: _____

NOTES ON MY DIG!

Question #: _____

NOTES ON MY DIG!

Question #: _____

NOTES ON MY DIG!

Question #: _____

NOTES ON MY DIG!

Question #: _____

NOTES ON MY DIG!

Question #: _____

NOTES ON MY DIG!

Question #: _____

NOTES ON MY DIG!

Question #: _____

NOTES ON MY DIG!

Question #: _____

NOTES ON MY DIG!

Question #: _____

NOTES ON MY DIG!

Question #: _____

NOTES ON MY DIG!

Question #: _____

NOTES ON MY DIG!

Question #: _____

NOTES ON MY DIG!

Question #: _____

NOTES ON MY DIG!

Question #: _____

90503677R00091

Made in the USA
Middletown, DE
24 September 2018